SECRETS
OF THE
SEASHORE

Carron Brown

Illustrated by Alyssa Nassner

Kane Miller
A DIVISION OF EDC PUBLISHING

A tide pool is bustling with life.

If you look closely between the rocks, beneath fronds of seaweed, and on the sandy bed, you will see the animals living there.

Shine a flashlight behind the page or hold it up to the light to reveal what is hidden in and around the tide pool. Discover a small world of great surprises.

A tide pool is a hollow
on the seashore.

Can you see what
happens when the tide
comes in?

Whoosh! The seawater flows
in with the tide and
fills the tide pool.

Creatures that live in seawater have waited for the tide pool to fill.

What's hiding in these shells?

Bubble...
   Bubble...

Mussels keep their blue shells tightly
shut while the tide is out.

Now they open their shells and begin to feed.

Creatures cling to the rocks around the pool.

Who could live in shells like these?

Barnacles come to life
in the water. They reach out
their feathery legs to wave
tiny pieces of food
into their mouth.

Flutter flutter

Other creatures are waking up, too.

What are these jewel-like animals?

Stretch!

Two sea anemones are searching for food with their long, wriggly tentacles.

They eat small fish and shrimp.

Dark nooks under rocks
make perfect hiding places.

Can you see who is resting here?

Click!

Click!

A crab holds its pincers up,
ready to grab a tidbit to eat.

The crab is on the move,
but there's another
hunter nearby.

Hold tight!

A starfish uses tubelike suckers on its underside to hold on to the rock.

Another animal with suckers
is resting in the tide pool.

Can you count its eight arms?

An octopus has eight long arms
with suckers on the underside.

It crawls slowly over the rocks.

There is an animal hiding in the sand.
Only its eyes can be seen.

What do you think it is?

Splish
Splash

A small fish lives in the tide pool.

It hides under rocks,
in seaweed, and in the sand.

Another tide pool creature
lives in this large shell.

What do you think it could be?

Surprise!

A hermit crab has made his home
in the empty shell.

This whelk is
sharing its part of the
tide pool with small
swimming creatures.

Can you see them?

Swish!

Shrimp move backward
by quickly flicking
their tails.

Their see-through bodies are much
easier to find when they move.

Something is
waving in the water.

Which plants live
in the sea?

Slick and slimy seaweed
anchors itself to rocks
and grows in the sun.

What is slithering along
in the seaweed?

A whelk is looking for other shellfish.

It can drill a hole through a shell to eat the creature inside.

A sleek sea otter has spotted something.

Can you see what she wants for dinner?

Ouch!

Most animals stay away
from those nasty spikes,
but a sea urchin is a tasty
meal for the sea otter.

Which orange-beaked bird
lives on the seashore?

An oystercatcher is
calling out to other birds.

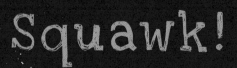

Squawk!

Can you see what the
oystercatcher has found
in the sand?

It's a clam!

The oystercatcher's long beak is perfect for finding buried food.

Slowly, the tide retreats,
and with it much of the
water in the tide pool.

Its animals and plants
are resting again, waiting
for the next tide to come in.

There's more...

When you find a tide pool, look all around it and see what you can find. Remember to look under the seaweed and in dark places.

In the sand Clams have a soft body inside two joined shells. They burrow under the sand and push a feeding tube into the water. Clams pull in their feeding tubes and snap their shells shut when they are in danger.

Stuck fast Whelks are sea snails that feed underwater. When the tide goes out, they pull their bodies into their shells. They seal themselves in with a sticky substance that also glues them to the rock.

In the cracks Crabs visit tide pools to feed on the other animals there. They catch them with their large pincers. Walking under seaweed and resting in cracks keeps crabs hidden from hungry birds.

From the air Gulls fly down to tide pools and catch shelled creatures in their beaks. They fly up high, then drop the shell onto rocks. This cracks the shell so that the birds can eat the soft meat inside.

Breaking in Sea otters grab sea urchins and shelled creatures from tide pools. To get at the meat inside, they float on their back with the caught animal on their tummy and use a stone to crack open the shell.

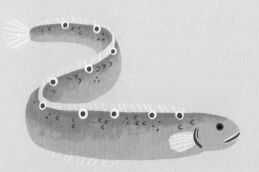

Trapped The fish in tide pools are often the young of larger fish that live in shallow seawater. They get trapped in the pools when the tide goes out. They hide in the sand, and under seaweed and rocks.

Holding on Seaweed anchors itself to rocks with a root-like holdfast. Its fronds float toward the surface of the tide pool, and make food from sunlight. Many tide pool animals feed on seaweed.

Changing color Octopuses can be hard to see because they can change color to match their surroundings. They can also position their bodies so that they look like rocks or the tide pool floor.

Filtering Lots of tide pool creatures get their food by filtering it from the seawater. Each time the rising tide refills the tide pool, it brings with it fresh nutrients and food for the creatures that live there.

First American Edition 2014
Kane Miller, A Division of EDC Publishing

Copyright © 2014 The Ivy Press Limited

For information contact:
Kane Miller, A Division of EDC Publishing
PO Box 470663
Tulsa, OK 74147-0663
www.kanemiller.com
www.edcpub.com
www.usbornebooksandmore.com

Library of Congress Control Number: 2013953406

Printed in China

ISBN: 978-1-61067-309-9